BORDERLINE

to nanny jan, thank you for always believing in me

I can't believe I'm here! I'm writing this for my first poetry book! Never in a million years did I think I would be in this place, writing has always been my world and I made it here. I've never been one to hide the fact I've struggled greatly with my mental health, at seventeen I was diagnosed with Borderline Personality Disorder and it has shook my world in so many ways. I wanted my first collection of poetry to represent that part of me, because I'm not ashamed and I refuse to hide it. This disorder is painful and breaks your very being, and naturally that shows in my writing. I write as an escape and most of the time it's my own head I'm running from, so rather than running, I've been writing and facing these thoughts. I want this poetry book to be a warm hug to others with BPD, and a place of insight for their loved ones. I have to warn it can be triggering at times, as these poems have come straight from my borderline brain and are unfiltered. I also want to point out the lack of capital letters in my poetry is intentional, I promise I'm not illiterate I just often write my poems in a rush to empty my brain onto a page and I like to keep it authentic to how it was originally created and this often means no capital letters or precise grammar, just pure vibes on a big page of brain soup.

Now, time for a depressing introduction to BPD and the poetry that waits ahead.

How it started

borderline personality disorder

Noun: PSYCHIATRY

1. a personality disorder characterised by severe mood swings, impulsive behaviour, and difficulty forming stable personal relationships.

I was seventeen when I was diagnosed with Borderline Personality Disorder, I had learnt what the disorder was a week before my diagnosis and spent my adolescence feeling alone and in therapy. I had friends, but they weren't like me. They all wore pretty clothes and played in the mud together whilst I watched wishing I had the courage to do so. They did so many fun activities, dancing, singing (I lost my ability to do any of those things around anybody in my life after the age of eight). I was sensitive, quiet, a crybaby, and quirky, at least that's what I was told by others around me. I didn't understand why it was unacceptable to cry when you're upset and why you were supposed to suppress it when other people got uncomfortable. I didn't understand the other children who behaved like their age and enjoyed barbies and teddies until now I'm twenty. I'm so unbelievably fixated on children's toys because of my lack of interest in them in childhood, but now I'm the weird one because what twenty year old collects dolls and stuffed animals… I was so focused on being a mature adult at the age of six to make sure everyone was safe and happy (I had no control over anything in my life and it broke me in an irreparable way).

I never felt in place as a child and now as an adult I feel even more helpless. Borderline is a sick and exhausting disease, I would give anything to be free from it for a day. If I had a day where I could live without my disorder I would go to a bar, I would make friends and have nice conversations without dumping my sad life story on them within the first five minutes and scaring them away, I would drink as much as I like and not worry about if I'm going to get addicted and reliant because when I wake up I feel like I'm a ghost watching my own body. A day of freedom, just a taste of mundane, a day where something as little as bumping my elbow on the door doesn't throw me off the rails for the next twenty four hours, I just desperately want to experience it. It's weird isn't it? When you ask people, especially children, what they would do if they could do or be anything they wanted for a day they would say things like

'I want to become the opposite gender for a day!'

'I want to become famous!'

'I would become the president!'

'I think I would become god!'

And I'm over here saying I want to feel like a normal human being… It's a bit sad to see that this is what this disorder has done to me, and I'm sure it's not just me who feels this way but in this very moment it truly feels like I am the only person on earth who does and it's lonely.

Fluoxetine Queen

harsh pills swallowed on a dry throat

it gets stuck to her tongue, just push it along

dreary eyes on cotton pillows

with a small crack of sunlight peaking her splintered floorboards

the whispers say

"close your eyes just a bit more"

she can't resist and falls a
sleeping corpse,

dopamine despaired dreams

filled with screeching and sins

she can't escape her thoughts
so she just lets them win,

the cotton sheets crumple as her
body crumbles

her mouth speaks words that are
hardly a mumble

the echos of a tummy rumble

digesting the powder she
requires to feel

and her silent snores bounce off
the walls, the only noise they get
to hear

the room spins and the wind
grazes her shins

so she takes her fluoxetine and
lets the cycle begin

Venus

when i ascend i hope venus
reaches for me

wraps me in her embrace and
gently closes my eyelids with her
merciful fingers

she'll wrap her hair around our
bodies

hold me tenderly and plant a
kiss on my cherry cheeks

we'll dance in the wind and sway
between clouds

she'll hold me tight and run her fingers through my hair like a waterfall of wine

our thighs will brush and our lips will hush as we observe the tweeting song birds that circle our hearts and heal our scars

her touch will heal me

and i'll fall apart

but in a magical way

my parts will scatter

and land in waterfalls on
mountains kissed by goddesses

Quiet Borderline

there is a rage in my soul

that screams to be released,

but i smother her mouth

even if little parts of her creep
through the cracks

Black Swan

my body has been cracking
since a few days old

haunted by memories i can't
even unfold,

the sounds

the sirens

dance delicately on my brain

the days where i feed them the
more they cause me pain,

they stop their fairy ballet

and turn it into a fierce rage

a black swan locked in a spiked cage counting down the rest of their days

piercing their feathers,

wasting a way

desperate to prove their mightiness before the day arrives

useless in the end

their bones are breaking and their body radiates pain

sobbing on the floor covered in blood and spit

but they went out doing it their way

Euphoria

12AM time to close my eyes

1AM twist and turn

2AM stare at the clock

3AM it's coming back

it's creeping on the brain like a money spider at midnight who spent the day hiding in the night light but crawls into your throat at the first sight of a slot with dimmed light,

it tickles in a way you can't
determine thorniness or
exhilaration;

the ability to convey with anyone
no matter the time of day or
spiral you may be in,

to declare worship to anyone
who looks your way and to sway
for the stars who don't know
your name

when you finally heave it out
there is destruction all around

just cobwebs half drowned

Chameleon Colours

my disposition paints me a
chameleon perched on a
multicoloured tree slowing falling
to an environmentally disastrous
death,

my tongue dry reaching for the
nearest diseased fly

my weight pushing down on a
shaved branch about the snap
from the weight of my brain
whilst my skin shifts at the sight
of a predator or prey,

i eulogise the transition in wind
to decide if i stay on a ticking
death trap or make a great
escape-

is it worth the energy

the waste of day

waste of life,

the cells pulsing through my
body can't decide which colour
represents me most from sage
to scarlet to soulless purple
whilst my mind goes over every
rainbow i've yet to inspect

i uncurl my tail

wrap my tongue

close my eyes

and embrace the fall

Indisposed

even when indisposed

i can light up any space i fill

and when i seek detriment

i must remind myself

i'm still intact no matter how
much weakness fills my bones

First!

rapid paws typing profusely on a cracked mirror

first!

notice me! /first

the desperate desire to be desired by strangers who will never understand why you desire them,

we pick at our skin, our bones, eyes and homes

why don't i have the same as the figure on the blue screen- i can see into her eyes and she would never recognise me

peoples voices echo through my living room,

voices of those who will never sit on this sofa or stand by my coffee table

but i'll still treat them as the guest of honour,

offer them tea and biscuits

hand them my two cents into
their relationship and politics

eventually they will fade away
with the sunset

a new voice every night
distracting me from whatever
mess is taking place in this
moment in time- in this section
of my life,

they won't remember by twelve
o'clock tomorrow what trauma i
spilled onto their laps just as
much as i wont be able to recall
what problems were in my cup
before it hit the floor

Please Recycle Me

everyone who has ever seen me

knows i am see-through,

translucent paper covered in
blood from paper cuts and
unfinished drawings nobody had
the guts to complete,

a slip of the finger

or the pressure of a pencil

could rip me in two

discard me for the rest of my existence

crumpled up

don't bother putting me in the recycling bin next to the cans and cardboard

just left to discompose

but i never actually do

you'll unfold me in a few years time

realise the drawing would've
been a masterpiece if you gave
the energy or the time

but it's too far now

too irrelevant at this point in your
life

so crumple me back up and
please, put me in the recycling
this time

Serial Arsonist

she can burn bridges made of
stone if you push her to,

she's a serial arsonist on the run

the law can't catch up and when
they do they fall in love

for she's not a criminal-

not an evil crook

just a girl desperate to feel truly
loved

Garden

there is a garden planted in your mind

that needs to be tended to with gentle care,

there will be rain along the way

but rain will allow you to grow,

open the doors to your greenhouse,

allow the water to flow

Defeat The Demons

if i defeat my demons

what will be left of me?

not even half a soul

just a swelling hole

Pocket Mirror

resent me for what i am;

refuse to acknowledge i am the
pocket mirror in your sleeve

all the darkness,

the death

that you saw in me

was a regurgitation of how you
were to me

Satisfied Itch

it starts as an itch

in her temple,

dreaming she can reach her slender fingers in

and stretch open the plucked skin

scratch until scarlet pours,

pull the cells out in such a rush it begins a downpour

further

deeper

strings of matter spread to the latter

an itch most satisfied

nothing else matters

Parallel Universe

maybe in a universe so parallel
nobody knows it exists,

and the occupants believe we
are just a rumour circulating
around space

no signs to indicate their
theories

there is a me-

who dances so unruffled she
lights the room

and at dusk

when the men surround
themselves with her scent;

she withdraws

for she is better than any of
them

Borderline

borderline

between what may i ask?

floating whilst the clock ticks by

tears on the night of your life

pain in pleasure

pleasure in pain

doors closed

the slams still echo in your brain

in-prisoned by your own name

dust scatters over where you lay

an endless impossible escape you planned at 5

imprints of those who held you tight

just to leave you in the night

sky's are blue but your mind is grey

it makes no sense why you feel this way

but at least you know borderline
is where you stay

there is safety in that pain

A Letter to My BPD

Dear BPD,

you weigh me down so much i fall to my knees

every inch of me is spread with you by a five inch butter knife everyone strives to clean but replaces out of bitterness when they sling it at the bin,

i just want to fathom why you insist on making me feel this way-

your constant urge to take over
my brain and lead me to the
worst mistakes,

ones that throw my life away and
lead me back to the start again

why would you take us back to
that place?

I should also ask,

why did you convince me my
lover was evil today when they
have been nothing but sunshine
in the way of the everlasting

tornado you insist we keep
spinning in-

my skin is splintered

my heels are calloused

my hands are raw

yet still you're preparing for us to
enter a war

one that could be over before it's
even begun but you already
loaded the gun,

you're an over supportive father
with abusive tendencies pushing

me to get a medal i never
wanted to yield

you know win or lose we will sit
in the bloody battlefield face
down with tears streaming down
scarlet hills covered in the
remains of the last ones we had
on our side

one day,

one absolutely miraculous day

you will leave my brain

you will leave my being

i will become whole

and it will feel so frigid without you but my god will it feel magnificent

just the thought of a chance that I can finally be free

from your cuffs and your screams

your horror will only live on in 80s VHS screens

eventually it will become history

a timeless classic, the tale of you and me

and i can't know that will be

but it's the most marvellous and magical dream

PART 2: FAVOURITE PERSON

Top Search Results:

"For someone with this type of BPD relationship, a "favourite person" is someone they rely on for comfort, happiness, and validation. The relationship with a BPD favourite person may start healthy, but it can often turn into a toxic love-hate cycle known as idealisation and devaluation."

A World Without You is Not a World

i don't want to live in a world
where your heartbeat isn't near

or on its way to caress mine

CORRUPTION

you tell all your friends

about how i was an inconvenience,

a manic imp at your disposal

but did you tell them about the corruption?

when my knees were bloody

and my eyes were sore

from pleading fidelity and nothing more.

Sensory Overload

he knows me better than the scars on my skin

but he doesn't know i listen for him

every bone crack

wrist snap

echos of his head being thrown back

his claps at the TV screen

or cries at sad movies,

the tip toe across the hallway
when i'm sleeping

slammed doors when his
strength in me is weakening,

every breath

heartbeat

sniffle

sneezing

jumping to excuse him

so he knows i'm always with him;

i have never liked sensory overload so much until i listened to him

and i would endure the loudest of frequencies just to be near him

Testosterone Filled Cups

the wave of eagerness leaves
my brain when i see the drooped
expression that sits on your
face,

the horror of listening to a
woman spew her liking for
something other than you is so
tragic and deafening you drown
it out and paint me the clown

i itch to tell you every word-

to share with you what makes
my world turn,

but it's nothing other than
weakness to your testosterone
filled cups-

always half full never willing to
walk to fill it up

instead i'll sew my lips shut and
contain the words trying to burst
out

for i know it won't cause your
fragility to burn out

Lungs

i do not enjoy the feeling

of missing your lungs

before the clock reaches lunch time

it feels like you've been gone for so long

even when every night you come to me with breath escaping your lungs

when you run home to give me a hug

i can't help but worry one day
you'll be gone

and i won't hear your struggling
lungs anymore

just silence as i long for you to
be here

Weed Killer

the love i hold for you
intertwines around my lungs like
weeds desperate to hold on,

no matter how much weed killer
i feed myself they still grow,

no tender care or expensive
tools will stop them growing,

they twist and wrap squeezing
the life out of me as they go
along

i try to water myself but they
draw it away,

feed themselves and leave me to dehydrate

their long arms reach for my scars

tear them open and watch me fall apart,

they don't even sprout on hearts of flower beds

just gravel and dust that's been left for dead

their roots grow deep

under the soil of my feet

muddy my body and make me
feel so weak

i think i found a sunflower

but a weed already killed it

the gardens unloved weeds have
destroyed me and my very being

Surrender

you dance with me like i am the
epitome of peace,

but my mind is a war machine
and you're my next opposition,

so i'll surrender before you leave
me to bleed

Motel of Mortals

stabbed awake in the motel of mortals

breath suctioned from the lungs like a shiny new hoover

blood baths half drained blocked by clots on the metal bowl

light of the half moon reflecting on a phone screen

reminiscence of tenderness on twisted bedsheets

echos of screeches ricocheted
across the stained glass
windows

cold linen stretches on the
threaded floor

their touch forevermore
engraved in the coppice door

Masterpiece

we are a masterpiece even if we
are a work in progress;

we have been anxiously painted
with fine lines and tender bristles
on a homemade canvas,

the palette is a mess

the walls are splattered red

but we will be a piece for the
history books ahead

What was the Question?

ask me again;

if i love you

after the sunsets

when my mind has shut off from the depth of the night and has had time to once again realise there is light

ask me again;

if i'll stay

after a fortnight of laying by my side

for every hour i spend with you i can't decide

ask me again;

why i'm leaving

if we had such a graceful time

and i'll tell you it's before you make the mistake to decide

Flesh Engraved Memories

my red raw flesh itches at the
memory of you

your cells meeting my own

my flesh will never be mine

it is stained red with your touch

when my flesh finally rots away

i will finally be my own

Tongue Twister

i sense its all going wrong from
the twist of your tongue

my limbs tighten

my eyes holding back the
waterfall bound to embark

i know it's coming

a sly remark

jab at my being

bringing back that awful
childhood feeling

the gravitational pull to the
bathroom floor

sink running so nobody hears
the fall

i've sobbed against each one of
your bathroom walls

Showstopper

if i told you

the things that swirl around my head in a steaming bowl of brain soup,

your head would fall off

maybe do a few spins before it drops;

implodes

do a slight bow before beginning the show

SHOUTING

it's easy to scribble lines about romance and heartbreak

but to have the urge to scribble in a hurry about love is a privilege everyone should be entitled to once in their life

and that's how i feel when i think about him

an overwhelming urge to tell the whole world

on paper

at the top of my lungs

Whipped cream

she never liked the taste of
security

until he handed it to her on a
shiny plate decorated with
dancing strawberries and
homemade whipped cream

Bloody Knees

my knees burn as you speak a
lie of the time i knelt on them at
your demise

do you believe i would ever ask
for you to be mine,

when you bled me dry and had
me beg for my life?

the scar you hide shows how i
possess your mind

tell them you had no choice
even though the thought of it
makes me lose my mind,

my stomach churns and my
chest hurts

thinking of all the lies you've told
whilst looking into peoples eyes

and how many trust your mind

believe you are a goddess
incapable of lies and i'm the
demon they should despise

i marked your life with my knife

and they won't understand how
you really stole my shine and
invaded my mind

but i'll know for the rest of my life who was the victim that escaped on a dime and you'll live knowing your perception of me is a lie

Fairy Land

meet me in an old oak tree

we will play hide and seek

until the sky turns pink,

we will take cover under the dripping toadstools

cuddle together as the rain falls

watch the daisies sway

and the fairy dust fly away

for as long as we stay

we know we are safe

Dust

never again will i open a wound

to fix another

my ribcage still aches

from every breath i spent on you

i'm glad my hands healed you

did you feel yourself drag the
energy from my brittle bones?

did you realise you emptied me?

the stars in my eyes dulled in the sight of the dust on your lungs

i allowed you to put me out like a cigarette and quit me when you were done

tell your friends about your dirty habit

even if in secret you are reaching for me

but you could never admit

you stole my shine

but still admire what you left of me

because i made you

and i am your very soul

you know i will never leave your being.

Off the meds again..

it's as if you're cursed with a
chronic need to disappoint me

and i'm supposed to accept it
and support you; as it is a
disease after all

but i'm getting tired of being a
symptom

please take your meds …

Printed in Great Britain
by Amazon